MW00680841

1/01

To My Baby
Luv - Yuv

Wisdom and Grace
Devotional Book for Young
Women of Color

Other Books for Women of Color:

Promises from God for Women of Color

The Wisdom and Grace Bible for Young
Women of Color

The Wisdom and Grace Devotional Bible
for Young Women of Color

The Women of Color Devotional

The Women of Color Devotional Bible

The Women of Color Journal

The Women of Color Study Bible

Wisdom and Grace Devotional Book

for Young Women of Color

A Devotional Created by and for
Contemporary Women of
African Descent

STEPHANIE PERRY MOORE
General Editor

WORLD
BIBLE PUBLISHERS, INC.
Iowa Falls, IA 50126 U.S.A.

World Publishing
Iowa Falls, IA

Nia Publishing
Atlanta, GA

Wisdom and Grace Devotional Book for Young Women of Color

© 2003 by Nia Publishing

NIA PUBLISHING is an African-American owned company based in Atlanta, GA. Started in 1993 by Mel Banks, Jr., former marketing director for Urban Ministries, Inc., its first product was *The Children of Color Bible*. Nia has recently produced the *Wisdom and Grace Bible for Young Women of Color* and the *Men of Color Study Bible*. The ownership, employees, and products of Nia Publishing are dedicated and committed to the cultural and spiritual growth of people of color, as individuals in the community and in the church. Nia can be visited on the internet at www.niapublishing.com.

Produced with the assistance of The Livingstone Corporation (www.LivingstoneCorp.com). Project staff includes: Carol Barnstable, Mary Horner Collins, Joan Guest, Kirk Luttrell, Anthony Platipodus, and Ashley Taylor.

This material has been taken from the *Wisdom and Grace Devotional Bible* © 2003 by Nia Publishing.

ISBN 0-529-11763-0 Hardcover

Published in cooperation with:
World Bible Publishers, Inc.
Iowa Falls, IA 50126
U.S.A.

Manufactured in the United States of America

1 2 3 4 5 6 7 8 DP 08 07 06 05 04 03

Contents

1. Thinking Positively   Jennifer Keitt   5
2. Amazing Love   Debra Nixon   9
3. Stand and Deliver   Monique Headley   13
4. Success   Vanessa Salami   17
5. Friendship   Chandra Sparks Taylor   21
6. Looks Aren't Everything   Regina Gail Malloy   25
7. Our Sin Nature   Michele Clark Jenkins   29
8. Abstinence   Yolanda Plunkett   33
9. The Sex Bandwagon   Torian Colon   37
10. Watch Your Tongue   Jazmyn Monet Childress   41
11. God's Plan   Winnie Clark-Jenkins   45
12. Freedom to Obey   Janet Meeks   49
13. Privacy   Ebony Lee   53
14. Are You a Slave?   Cynthia Brawner   59
15. God Loves You   Jacquelin McCord   61
16. Will You Pass or Fail?   Sabrina Black   65
17. Free to Be Me?   Wanda Kimball   69
18. Marriage First   Anita Daniels   73
19. Grandma's Traditions   Vickie Wilson   77
20. Just As I Am   Ramona Tillman   81
21. Give Your Parents a Break!   Nicole Smith   85
22. Heeding Instructions   Christina Dixon   89
23. We Are Family   Eva Jenise Gibson   93
24. Try Contentment   Chandra Sparks Taylor   97

25. Better Than Wine — Marlow Talton 101
26. God Hates Sin — Jamell Meeks 105
27. Hanging Out — Tammy Garnes 109
28. Healthy Lifestyle — Patrice Elliot-Mace 113
29. Committed — Portia Lee 117
30. Lost and Found — Eloise Averhart 121
31. Transforming Your Thoughts — Edythe Thomas 125
32. Mind Choices — Pamela Hudson 129
33. Lead by Example — Kim Bailey 133
34. Walking by Faith — Pamela Rollins 137
35. The Test — Veronica Alexander 141
36. Quiet Time — Marilyn Turner 145
37. What's a Church? — Gwen Coates 149
38. God's Beauty Mark — Laverne Hall 153
39. Joy — Marsha Woodard 157
40. Kindness — Nicole Bailey Williams 161
41. Peace — Adell Dickinson 165
42. Control Yourself — Karen Waddles 169
43. Real Knowledge — Chandra Dixon 173
44. Single and Whole — Raykel Tolson 177
45. Temptation — Francis Jefferson 181
46. The Master Planner — Cherrill Wilson 185
47. Serving God — Michele Clark Jenkins 189
48. Another Chance — Patricia Heggler 193
49. The Promised Gift — Rachelle Hollie Guillory 197
50. How's Your Vision? — Trevy McDonald 201

Thinking Positively

JENNIFER KEITT

And be not conformed to this world:
but be ye transformed by the renewing
of your mind, that ye may prove
what is that good, and acceptable,
and perfect, will of God.

Romans 12:2

Renew Your Mind

"I just don't think I can do it," Lisa moaned to her friend, Kelley.

"Sure you can, girl, just practice these moves with me and you can make the squad!"

"Kelley, you're always so sure and positive about things. Why is that?" Lisa questioned.

"Well, my mom always told me that we can do anything that we think we can do, so I think I can do it all, girl!"

"Wow," Lisa said, "I always think I can't do anything."

....

There is a brand-new life waiting for you right between your ears! Researchers say that human beings think, on average, 50,000 thoughts a day. That's more than one thought per second. If you're spending that time thinking negatively, you're going to have a rotten, negative life. But if you start thinking about God's positive ways and the great things that he has for you, you can have a better life. Guess what? You'll have all that God wants for you!

God is so awesome that he has created and wired us to do and have great things in our lives. He tells us plainly how to change: "And be not conformed to this world: but be ye transformed by the renewing of your mind" (Romans 12:2). Change comes when you make the quality decision to consciously change how you're thinking. Do you always imagine the worst? Are you always struggling with feeling that you're not good enough, strong enough, cute enough, or popular enough? Then check your thinking. Whatever you're thinking in your heart, that's what you are or will become. God wants you to be an awesome woman. You can be, if you think and believe that you can!

Changing your thinking is truly as easy as 1-2-3, but it will take some consistency and determination to see your brand-new life! Let's get started.

Application

Try putting these steps into action today: 1) Decide that you want to change for the right reasons—to please God. 2) Understand that change always takes time, so don't be in a hurry. The transformation from Ms. Negativity to Ms. Positivity is going to take some well-spent time. 3) Use the Bible as your main resource for changing your thinking. The Bible says, "This book of the law shall not depart out of thy mouth; but thou shalt meditate therein day and night, . . . for then thou shalt make thy way prosperous, and then thou shalt have good success" (Joshua 1:8).

Prayer

Father, help me to think like you! I want to think your thoughts. Help me to change my outlook, to think positive thoughts, and to view my life the way you view it. In Jesus' name. Amen.

Amazing Love

DEBRA NIXON

For God so loved the world,

that he gave his only begotten Son,

that whosoever believeth in him

should not perish,

but have everlasting life.

John 3:16

Just Accept It

Charlotte sat in youth Bible study as the teacher told the story of Nicodemus, who came to ask Jesus a question about salvation. In the story, Jesus told Nicodemus that he needed to know God in a different way if he was going to be in a close relationship with God. Jesus told the man: "For God so loved the world, that he gave his only begotten Son, that whosoever believeth in him should not perish, but have everlasting life."

This was news to Nicodemus—and to Charlotte! No one had ever explained that she could come to God through Jesus, and that it was because of God's love that one received salvation. She had always thought of God as someone who punished "bad" children by letting the devil get them. She figured that if a grown man like Nicodemus could start all over with God, surely she could. She asked her teacher how she could be saved. Her teacher responded, "Accept God's love through Jesus by believing in him in your heart."

God loved you so much that he gave innocent Jesus to die for your guilt. That's an awesome love. Do you know anyone who loves you so much that they would die for you? The Bible says that God willingly gave Jesus, and Jesus willingly gave his life so that you can experience the love of God and have a personal relationship with God through Jesus. The Bible says that Jesus is the only way to know God. Just think—all you have to do to receive the salvation of God is believe on Jesus' name.

Application

If you have not experienced the awe of God's love, decide right now that you will. For the next five days, in addition to your regular prayers, pray the words of John 3:16.

Prayer

God of our salvation, you have loved us with an unmatched love. I accept this love and ask Jesus into my heart. Keep showing me your love in the days to come, as I am young and sometimes the message of your love gets lost. Thank you, Jesus. Amen.

Stand and Deliver

MONIQUE HEADLEY

Then said I, Ah, Lord GOD! behold,

I cannot speak: for I am a child.

But the LORD said unto me, Say not, I am a

child: for thou shalt go to all that I shall send thee,

and whatsoever I command thee thou shalt speak.

Be not afraid of their faces: for I am with thee to

deliver thee, saith the LORD.

Jeremiah 1:6-8

Fight or Flee

As the only committed Christian on the Valentine's Day Dance planning committee, Riley felt dejected after the last meeting. The committee wanted to make the dance a purely fun event, complete with a shake-what-ya-mama-gave-ya dance contest. Riley felt it would be more appropriate if the event wasn't so wild, but instead included an abstinence pledge ceremony.

The other students didn't want to give her idea much weight, and Riley felt unsure of how to change their minds. Faced with the decision to quit or stay on and try to persuade the other students, Riley was at a crossroads. Her decision would have an impact on how she would be perceived and received. On behalf of the Lord, would her decision be to fight or take flight?

Our honest responses and decisions say more about our personal convictions than our words, for they reveal our beliefs with crystal clarity. Life will provide plenty of opportunities for such revelations. How are we to respond? Are we to profess the glory of the Lord only when we know it will be easily received, and be silent when we know we might have to explain our beliefs? It is important that we fight the good fight—always—not according to convenience. The power of the Lord will guide you to where you are supposed to be, when you are supposed to be there, and instruct you on what you are supposed to do and say. Our mamas know what they gave us, and I bet they never wanted it to be shaken. Tell somebody what you know about the goodness of the Lord.

Application

When you are faced with a challenging situation in which others are not open to your Christian ideals, take the time to speak with them one-on-one. Respect their opinions, but tell how Jesus has changed your life and how they could benefit from the same gift. If you find yourself in a situation of unconscionable compromise, find communion with other like-minded Christian women and hold on to your faith.

Prayer

Lord, guide me on my journey and give me the strength to spread your Word as far as possible. I will listen for your words so that I may reach those outside the brilliance of your light. I love you, Lord. Amen.

Success

VANESSA SALAMI

And David behaved himself wisely

in all his ways; and the LORD

was with him.

1 Samuel 18:14

Sold Out to God

Mariah and Arielle stepped down from their ride, dancing, singing, and blowing kisses to the city bus as it pulled away. Arielle stopped and hugged her friend, "You did it! I am so proud of you! You are the girl!"

Mariah and Arielle were returning from an audition for an upcoming play, I Did It God's Way. Mariah had gotten the lead role. Mariah was sad that her best friend did not get a part, but Arielle was not the least bit mad, sad, or jealous. She was very happy for Mariah, who had faced a lot of pressure at school and at home, but still managed to get good grades, be active in the youth ministry at church, and live up to her responsibilities.

Mariah said that she started each day by greeting God and asking him to lead her in everything that she would do during the day. On this day, Mariah knew God was doing more than leading her and Arielle; he was playing the music to which they were dancing and singing.

Just as David was a man after God's own heart, God is searching the earth today for those whose hearts are sold out to him. Young women whose hearts are filled with the love of God are rare jewels today. Because God is with such young ladies, they will find success in all that they do. Their light will draw others who will want to know what the secret to these young women's glow is.

Television tells young people that success is about who you know; you have to know the "right people" to get discovered. Television has half the story right. True success, the kind that lasts for all eternity, is about knowing and living for the right somebody—the one true God.

Application

It is time to find out who or what is captivating your heart. Get seven sheets of paper. Label each sheet a different day of the week. Divide each sheet into three sections, for morning, afternoon, and evening. Then jot down the very first thoughts that come to your mind one morning, what you focus on during the middle of the day, and what things occupied your heart in the evening. After one week, read all the sheets and determine whether you need to ask God to clean your heart and mind so that he is the major focus of your life.

Prayer

Lord, thank you for being my Father and my friend. Thank you for making a way for me to be successful by loving you with all my heart. In the name of the King of Kings. Amen.

Friendship

CHANDRA SPARKS TAYLOR

Faithful are the wounds of a friend;

but the kisses of an enemy

are deceitful.

Proverbs 27:6

Friends Indeed

From the moment Nia and Jessica met in seventh grade, they were inseparable. They ate lunch together and talked on the phone every night. When you saw one, you saw the other—until they had an argument about Jessica's cheerleading routine and stopped speaking.

One day Jessica found Nia crying in the bathroom. Forgetting their argument, she quickly went to comfort her friend. "What's wrong, Jess?"

"I found out today that I made the cheerleading squad."

"That's great," Nia said, truly happy for her friend. "Why are you crying though?"

"Well, I was so excited when I got the news, I couldn't wait to tell you. But then I remembered that we weren't talking. I just got so mad at myself. When I had asked your advice about my routine and you gave me your honest opinion, I didn't want to hear that I was a little stiff. You were right, Nia, and I knew it. I took your advice, and now look at me; I made the squad. But I feel horrible because I lost my best friend in the process."

"Girl, please, you cannot get rid of me that easily. I was hurt, but I prayed that God would restore our friendship, and he has. Now we have two things to celebrate—your making cheerleader and our friendship!"

True friends will not tell you what you want to hear; they will tell you the truth, no matter how much it hurts. Although you may not always want to hear it, knowing that someone is going to be there for you—no matter what you are going through—is comforting. True friendship, like true love, stands the tests of time. Make sure that you choose wisely when you choose your friends.

Application

Today make a list of all of your friends. Examine your list honestly and eliminate all those who have talked about you behind your back, lied to you, laughed about you, or done things that were not in your best interest. How many people are left? Most people are lucky if they have one real friend. Regardless of how many people are still on the list, take the time today to write each one a short note or send an E-mail thanking them for their friendship.

Prayer

Lord, thank you for surrounding me with people who love and care about me in spite of my faults. Bless me to be the kind of friend I want others to be to me. In thy Son's name I pray. Amen.

Looks Aren't Everything

REGINA GAIL MALLOY

But the LORD said unto Samuel,

Look not on his countenance,

or on the height of his stature;

because I have refused him:

for the LORD seeth not as man seeth;

for man looketh on the outward appearance,

but the LORD looketh on the heart.

1 Samuel 16:7

What God Sees

"Shaundra! Look who's on the cover of Black Enterprise *magazine. Jeremy Picolo! He's one of the richest young men under 30!" Cheryl exclaimed.*

"You mean old Pic'n Pay from high school?" Shaundra cried. "I mean, he was nice and all, but he was such a nerd!"

"Well, honey, he ain't Pic'n Pay no more. Look! He's Picked and Paid!" Cheryl said, laughing. "He's also the same guy who asked you to the prom, but you told him no because you thought Trey was soooo fine!"

"Don't even remind me!" Shaundra exclaimed. "Trey was so arrogant and rude. I don't know what I ever saw in him. The boy couldn't even read. Oh, I'm so mad I could kick myself! Who would have thought that Pic—I mean, Jeremy—would turn out to be a millionaire!"

....

We all know at least one: the boy who's usually smart but not very popular or attractive. The guys who are really fine looking are the ones who get the attention. However, the Bible tells us that God is not concerned about how we look on the outside; he's concerned about our hearts and our thoughts. When you're looking at a boy, don't just look at his dimples or his eyes. Find out what's in his heart;

that will reveal the kind of person he really is. "For as he thinketh in his heart, so is he" (Proverbs 23:7).

Application

Think about one guy whom you find attractive. Write down three things that make him attractive. Then, based on Proverbs 23:7, write down three things about him that God would consider important. Compare the two lists. If the lists match, wonderful; if not, begin looking at others the way God does.

Prayer

Dear Lord, I'm so thankful you don't look at us in the way that we look at ourselves. You see us for who we really are deep down. Lord, please help me to see others the way you see them. In Jesus' name, I pray. Amen.

Our Sin Nature

MICHELE CLARK JENKINS

For they that are after the flesh

do mind the things of the flesh;

but they that are after the Spirit

the things of the Spirit. . . .

So then they that are in the flesh

cannot please God.

Romans 8:5,8

Queen of Her Life

At 14 years old, Carolyn was already experimenting with boys. Her parents were aware of what was going on and tried to cut her off from the "bad influences." What's the big deal? *she thought.* It was her body and her choice.

The real problem was that Carolyn was her own bad influence. In her mind anything she felt like doing, any time she felt like doing it, was okay. No boundaries. She'd already tried smoking and drinking. Didn't like the cigarettes much, but loved to drink beer. She was queen of her own kingdom. She ruled her own world.

....

Ever since the Garden of Eden, when Adam and Eve disobeyed God, we've inherited a sin nature. The King James Version of the Bible calls it "the flesh." Without boundaries based on God's Word and our civil laws, we tend to do any old thing because we feel like it at the moment. Living by the flesh comes naturally.

Until we are able to decide on our own what set of principles we will live by, our parents have to protect us from ourselves. Your parents hope that you will live by the values they have taught you. The world is made up of many people who do what their flesh tells them to do. That's the opposite of what God would have you do.

Application

Think about what you would do differently in your life if your parents weren't around, or they all of a sudden lost their minds and told you there were no more rules. Do you think that without supervision you'd be living your life God's way?

Prayer

Lord, I see that I am imperfect and that my flesh tugs on me every day to do only what feels good. Lord, I am trusting the Holy Spirit to show me a better way, a way that will please you. Amen.

Abstinence

YOLANDA PLUNKETT

Thou wilt keep him in perfect peace,

whose mind is stayed on thee.

Isaiah 26:3

Under Pressure

Yvonne was fast approaching her senior year in high school. She had managed to resist the peer pressure to smoke, drink, and have sex. Yvonne never had any interest in having sex, even though all of her friends were doing it and told her how much fun they were having. But Yvonne knew in her heart that pre-marital sex was wrong and tried to steer clear of any situations that might tempt her.

But now the pressure was on. One Saturday night Yvonne met the guy of her dreams at a basketball game. William was gorgeous and treated her like a queen. She got butterflies in her stomach every time he entered the room. Yvonne and William dated for about six months and became closer than ever, but she noticed that he was starting to want more physically than she was willing to give. Yvonne was in love with William and didn't want to lose him. She knew, despite her emotions and hormones, that she would have to make a decision that would not go against her (and her family's) moral values.

The choice not to have sex before marriage and to remain abstinent is a tough decision to make. The media, movies, and music make it almost impossible to stay focused on purity. When you are confused and unsure, you can be pressured easily into going against your beliefs. Your mind must be stayed on God and his Word. "Trust in the LORD with all thine heart; and lean not unto thine own understanding" (Proverbs 3:5).

It is right to say, "No, I'm not ready yet." Even better, say that you are saving your virginity for marriage. When you respect yourself, others will respect you as well. Losing someone because we choose to do what is right can be painful. When the pressure is on, turn to God, stay in prayer, and he will help you through those difficult times.

Application

For one week choose not to engage in any situation that may cause you to feel uncomfortable or tempted sexually. If there is a song of a sexual nature on the radio, turn it off. Don't watch any music videos or television programs with sexual content. Only attend movies that are wholesome and educational. Say no to explicit conversations with your girlfriends. Meditate on God's Word and pray, asking God for strength and direction. After one week, acknowledge how refreshed and stress free you are. Give God the praise!

Prayer

Lord, you are the center of my joy, and no one will come before you. Help me to remember that my body is a temple that is not meant for sexual immorality but for the Lord's glory. Amen.

The Sex Bandwagon

TORIAN COLON

For ye are bought with a price:

therefore glorify God in your body,

and in your spirit, which are God's.

1 Corinthians 6:20

Respect Your Body

Eboni was feeling pressure from her friends and her boyfriend about having sex. The subject was driving her crazy because she knew everyone around her was sexually active. Mason, her boyfriend of a year and a half, was ready to take their relationship to the "next level." He was tired of having a girl who was only willing to kiss and hold hands. He was ready for an intimate, sexual relationship.

"Look, Eboni," her friend Karla said, "Jason and I have been making love since we were fifteen, and we're almost seventeen now, and I haven't had any complaints. I know he loves me."

Eboni looked at her friend, "Jason flirts with other girls and he says rude things to you. If being disrespected is showing love, then I don't want it."

"There you go with the goody-two-shoes stuff again," Karla lectured. "You better jump on the bandwagon, girl, so you can keep your man. This is the new millennium." Karla went to the bathroom and Eboni remembered her Sunday school teacher's verse from the previous week: "For ye are bought with a price: therefore glorify God in your body, and in your spirit, which are God's" (1 Corinthians 6:20).

"You know what, Karla?" Eboni said when her friend returned. "You need to jump off that sex bandwagon and

jump onto God's. Your body is his, not Jason's, and personally, I'd rather glorify God by showing him I respect the body he gave me by not taking part in any sexual activities. I'm just not interested."

....

Are you a leader or a follower? If you're a leader, then you will allow God's Word to work through you and get you through testing situations. In life, we are tested, but we can pass those tests if we follow God, not other people. God wants his children to be readers and leaders of his Word.

Application

Make a list of friends that you may need to encourage to jump on to God's bandwagon with you. Stand firm in what you believe and don't fall prey to peer pressure. Your friends may try to encourage you to jump on to their worldly bandwagon, but you have to stand firm on God's Word.

Prayer

Lord, thank you for friends and relationships, but help me to stay focused on my relationship with you. I don't want to lean on them for support, Lord; I only want to lean on you. Amen.

Watch Your Tongue!

JAZMYN MONET CHILDRESS

A soft answer turneth away wrath:

but grievous words stir up anger.

Proverbs 15:1

Guard Your Words

April was talking on the phone to a friend from school when the conversation turned into gossip. The girl started telling April some mean and nasty things that another girl in their group had said about her.

April was shocked and hurt. For a minute April thought about calling the girl to give her a piece of her mind, but she knew that would only stir up more confusion. April knew it was her responsibility to use wisdom and knowledge so that she could be an example in this situation. Instead of calling the girl and making the situation worse, April decided to calm down and pray. She waited until the next day to handle the situation in a much more mature and godly manner.

Living in the flesh, we face temptation every day. But living in the spirit is easy if we obey the Word of God. As women of God, we must pray and ask the Lord to guide us regarding what we should say and when we should say it. Before the telephone rings we should ask the Lord to guard our tongues, the words we use, and the topics that we discuss with others.

This also applies to our everyday life in conversations with friends, family, and colleagues. The Bible says, "The tongue of the wise useth knowledge aright: but the mouth of fools poureth out foolishness" (Proverbs 15:2). We want to represent God well. We need to use the Bible as the guide for our lives and use our tongues to share his wisdom and knowledge, rather than to say foolish things that are not of God.

Application

When you come across a situation when something negative has been said about you, just pray. Don't try to work out the problem by yourself and make the situation worse. Be responsible. Keep in mind that the Lord knows best and that he will fight every one of your battles for you.

Prayer

Lord, I need you to guide me and help me watch what I say to people. I am responsible for what I say and do. I want to be able to say the right words at the right time. Fill my mouth with love and wisdom. Let your Holy Spirit take control of my tongue and the things that I say to others. In Jesus' name, I pray. Amen.

God's Plan

WINNIE CLARK-JENKINS

for this cause have I raised thee up,
for to shew in thee my power;
and that my name may be declared
throughout all the earth.

Exodus 9:16

God's Plan

Dawn was a senior in high school. With graduation coming, she thought about her future and the changes that would be made in her life when she went off to college. All of Dawn's friends were stressed out, but Dawn was not. She had the peace of God. She knew that he had a plan for her life and would not let her go astray, since God was her top priority. Her friends couldn't help but ask why she seemed to take her future in stride. It was Dawn's chance to tell her friends that God had a plan for their lives, too.

Sometimes we let things of the world stress us out, but we have nothing to fear if God is our top priority. God is good! God has a plan for our lives. Since we serve a good God, then he must have good plans for us. Knowing that God has a plan for us, we can be at peace. Our peace with God's plan for us should also encourage us to share his plan with others.

Application

Today, go right to the source and ask God what his plans are for your life. Be sure that you not only ask, but that you take time to listen.

Prayer

Lord God, I love you so much and I want to serve you the rest of my life. Please lead and guide me through my life and help me to keep on the path you have made for me. Amen.

Freedom to Obey

JANET MEEKS

Children, obey your parents in all things:

for this is well pleasing unto the Lord.

Colossians 3:20

When Mom Isn't Around

Wynter was told by her mother not to wear makeup to school. "Please, Mom," Wynter pleaded, "all the other girls have some on."

Her mother said firmly, "Do I look like somebody who cares about what everybody else is doing?" Placing her arms around Wynter, her mother said, "Sweetie, we'll talk about it for next year in high school. But for now, trust me that I know what's best."

Wynter agreed to follow her mom's decision. However, when she got to school, her girlfriends tried to pressure her into wavering. "Girl, yo' mama ain't here," one friend said. "Put it on, you'll look great," prodded another.

Wynter decided to abide by her mom's wishes. When the girls stepped out of the bathroom, only Wynter got a compliment from the cutest guy in school.

Wynter's friends were right. Her mother couldn't see what she was doing in school. However, Wynter wanted to please her mother and God, so she chose to obey, and got a blessing for doing so. God has given us many rules in his Word to abide by. It is up to us to follow them. We have the freedom to obey or not to obey. Make sure you obey every time.

Application

If you have a friend who is going against her parents' wishes, encourage her to abide by the rules and not to break them.

Prayer

God, following your rules is not easy sometimes. Following my parents' rules isn't easy either. However, it is written in your Word that "I can do all things through Christ which strengtheneth me" (Philippians 4:13). Help me lean on your strength to do what is right. Amen.

Privacy

EBONY LEE

For in the time of trouble

he shall hide me in his pavilion:

in the secret of his tabernacle

shall he hide me;

he shall set me up upon a rock.

Psalm 27:5

Talking to God

Lynette has no privacy because she shares a room with her little sister. Her little sister sees everything that Lynette does—even when she is getting dressed. It's hard to have privacy with a little sister around.

Not only does Lynette's little sister see everything but she also tells everything. Her little sister cannot keep a secret and that really makes privacy hard. All someone has to do is to give her a little money and she'll tell on Lynette. Sometimes Lynette locks herself in the bathroom or sneaks into her brother's room and hides when he's not there, just so she can be alone.

We all want to have privacy for ourselves—privacy to talk on the telephone, to listen to music, or just to be alone when we need to be. Sometimes you can't get privacy. So what do you do? You get in touch with your inner self by talking to God. God will protect you when you share with him. Just talk to him instead of trying to hide your feelings or your problems. Some people may not understand you, but God always understands you.

Application

If you need privacy or need someone to talk to, get by yourself and pray. Just try it. (Never say you can't, because trying counts for something.) If you have a problem, do something about it. Get in the tub to relax your body and pray, and just stay there for a few minutes and listen to God. He will help you.

Prayer

Lord, I come to you with my desire for privacy. I have little sisters and brothers who are too young to understand. Sometimes I need to be alone and I need you to help me with it, because I can't help myself without you. Amen.

Are You a Slave?

CYNTHIA BRAWNER

And the LORD said, I have surely seen

the affliction of my people which are in Egypt,

and have heard their cry by reason of their

taskmasters; for I know their sorrows;

And I am come down to deliver them out of the

hand of the Egyptians, and to bring them up out

of that land unto a good land.

Exodus 3:7,8

Trapped by Trends

The children of Israel were God's chosen people. He provided everything for them. Yet they found themselves trapped in slavery to the Egyptians for four hundred years. They were forced to serve a Pharaoh who did not believe in God and who feared their population growth. Even with all their sorrows, when God was delivering them out of Egypt, they were afraid to give up what they knew. "It had been better for us to serve the Egyptians, than that we should die in the wilderness," they cried.

Our lives are similar to those of the children of Israel, by the way we "serve" others or things. Think about it. Are you in some type of bondage? Do you find yourself following the trends of the world by participating in body piercing or permanent body painting? Do you feel that you must wear the latest hair and clothing styles? Are you a slave to peer pressure?

There is only one God and he is not concerned about our outward appearance. He is concerned with our inward appearance, the eternal security of our souls. You'll never be disappointed if you serve him.

Application

Check yourself. Are you trapped in bondage as the children of Israel were? Start living a life for God and let your outward Christian values show. Cover the inside of your locker door with reminders of Jesus Christ. Open up to a new way of thinking and behaving.

Prayer

Father God, in the name of Jesus, I ask that you deliver me from darkness and place me into your marvelous light. Cleanse me and help me be a slave to you, living my life dedicated to you. Amen.

God Loves You

JACQUELIN MCCORD

Nor height, nor depth,

nor any other creature,

shall be able to separate us

from the love of God,

which is in Christ Jesus

our Lord.

Romans 8:39

God's Love Is Enough

Travis was 17 years old and a junior in high school. He had transferred to this school, but quickly got involved. He was on the football, chess, and debate teams, in the gospel choir and boy scouts. One Friday evening Travis was home doing his homework. When he was done, he neatly stacked his books and papers on the table. Then he climbed on top of the kitchen table and hanged himself.

The school was devastated, shocked, and hurt. They wondered, "Why would someone who had such a bright future do something like that?" There was another side to Travis's life many people were unaware of. When his parents divorced, Travis had been sent to Chicago to live with relatives in the public housing projects. Travis had hated living in these circumstances and suffered in silence. At his funeral the minister said, "As we sit here today, wiping the tears from our eyes and trying to find ways to understand why Travis, a young man who meant so much to so many, would take his own life, there is only one explanation, . . . Travis didn't know that God loved him."

How many times have you shared a heartfelt problem with someone, only to be told, "God loves you"? People say it so much that the words have become almost meaningless, without any real understanding of your problems. But think about it. Is God's love enough when you are hurting? I encourage you to read what the Scriptures say about God's love for you. Whatever you do, don't give up on God; he loves you too much. One thing you can count on is that nothing can separate his children from his love.

Application

Start a prayer group with some of your friends from school. Be there for one another and seek to have honest heartfelt dialogue while encouraging each other in prayer.

Prayer

Father, you are the God of love. Sometimes I feel as if no one loves me. I know that you love me. Help me to feel your love, Lord, so that when things get me down, I won't feel so sad. Amen.

Will You Pass or Fail?

SABRINA BLACK

Not rendering evil for evil,

or railing for railing:

but contrariwise blessing;

knowing that ye are thereunto called,

that ye should inherit a blessing.

1 Peter 3:9

The Grace Test

Veronica was in shock when Renita left her a voice-mail message about Renita's failing math grade. What happened? Could this really be true? Not straight-As-eversince-kindergarten Renita, Veronica thought happily. It's about time she failed at something.

Since kindergarten, Renita had always outdone Veronica in everything, and she usually made a point of boasting about it. Now she could give Renita a taste of her own medicine. Veronica knew that her response was not right, but it was so tempting. She had barely passed math herself, with a C. But now that C seemed as if it were a good grade in comparison. Veronica thought all day about what she would say when she called Renita back.

As she played the message again, a Bible verse came to mind. Veronica knew that she should not render evil for evil but be a blessing instead (1 Peter 3:9). Yes, she could try to teach Renita a lesson, but right now Renita needed comfort, encouragement, and a good math tutor.

....

Have you ever had to resist the temptation to teach someone a lesson? Think for a moment about the situation. What did you do? Did you pass or fail "the grace test?" Were you able to recall any Scriptures to encourage you to make the right choice?

The Scripture is clear—when someone is wrong, don't throw it in their face. (The same thing could happen to you.) Instead, look for ways you can help them. Thank God that Veronica remembered God's Word and chose to apply it in her life. You might want to do the same thing. Whenever you are faced with a tough decision, God's Word can provide direction. It takes the grace of God to pass "the grace test" and make the right choice, being supportive of others.

Application

Veronica had a list of Renita's offenses that went all the way back to preschool. Are you keeping track of the wrongs that others have done? As you shower them with grace, you will let it go and love them in spite of their faults. Identify one person whom you have something against and ask God to forgive you. Then do something nice for that person.

Prayer

Lord, how great is the temptation to get back at those who belittle us when we fail! Help us to be gracious in our attitudes. Thank you for always reminding us that we are all subject to falling. And thank you for being there to pick us up and place us on the right path. Amen.

Free to Be Me?

WANDA KIMBALL

And she said unto her,

All that thou sayest unto me I will do.

And she went down unto the floor,

and did according to all

that her mother in law bade her.

Ruth 3:5,6

Choose to Obey

"My mother doesn't tell me what to do. I do what I want!"
Vaughna said while talking to her friends in her bedroom.

"Vaughna!"

"Yes, ma'am?"

"Come down and help me with these groceries."

"I'm coming." Vaughna smiled as she looked back at
her friends. "I'm only doing it because I want to do it."

....

Adolescence is an exciting time when physical,
emotional, and social changes are taking place. Like
budding flowers, girls develop into beautiful, young
women. Clothing, hairstyle, and even nail-color
choices are seen as defining an individual. Boys are
categorized as "cute" or "yucky." The big circle of
childhood friends grows smaller.

Parents allow more space to make your own
choices and to do your own thing.

Ruth, a young woman in the Old Testament,
had an opportunity to go her own way and make
her own lifestyle. When her husband died, she
could have chosen to go back to her homeland. Yet
she chose to stay with her mother-in-law, Naomi.
Ruth asked Naomi's advice about how to handle
herself at work. She could have done things her
way, but she accepted Naomi's guidance. God

blessed her obedience, and she eventually became King David's ancestor.

Growing into womanhood does not always guarantee doing what you want. It does not totally free you from obeying authority. Obedience to parents forms a pattern for following teachers, bosses, and other leaders. Ultimately, obedience teaches us to follow God. God gave us the free will to obey or not to obey. Our choices can bring blessings or curses.

Application

Today, remember that God has given you freedom to be yourself, but has also placed people in authority over you. Do what you are told without talking back. If you do not understand, politely ask questions. Ask God to help you to be obedient when you are asked to do something that you do not like to do. Being obedient to those in charge brings peace and blessings in your life.

Prayer

Heavenly Father, thank you that I am learning to be a responsible young adult by following directions. When I do as I am told, I know that I am also obeying you. In Jesus' name, I pray. Amen.

Marriage First

ANITA DANIELS

But from the beginning of the creation

God made them male and female.

For this cause shall a man leave his father

and mother, and cleave to his wife.

Mark 10:6,7

The Order of Things

Fifteen-year-old Mia was chatting with her best friends, Tiffany and Shaunessay. Shaunessay said, "I know I don't have a boyfriend, but I need to find someone to have a couple of babies with before I get married—maybe have my first after I turn sixteen."

Tiffany chimed in, "Yeah, if you prove to him that you love him by giving him a baby, he's sure to ask you to be his girlfriend and marry you after graduation."

Mia was so surprised by the dialogue between her friends that she had to ask, "But what if he doesn't ask you to marry him? You'll have two babies and no husband."

Shaunessay replied, "But that's the only way you can make sure you'll get married, by having his baby now. Mia, you'd better be thinking about who you want your baby's daddy to be."

The Pharisees and Jesus' disciples often questioned Jesus about marriage and how God wants marriage to work. Jesus explained to them that God has an expected order for relationships. Many young women are having babies before they get married. It is not clear why this phenomenon appears to be the "in" thing, but it is not the way of God.

Making and having a baby are not the steps one has to take in order to get married. It is clear in Genesis 2 that God created Adam's wife. Eve did not meet Adam at the altar already bearing his children, because she wasn't trying to "find and hook a man." God was solely responsible for choosing Eve for Adam.

Application

Write down what you think the Bible says about God's expectations for marriage. Using the concordance of your Bible, find, read, and analyze a Scripture about marriage every day for the next five days. At the end of each day, write down the new information you've learned.

Prayer

Dear God, my friends and I are often confused about the topic of marriage. I see and hear so many different messages. Teach me your standards for marriage and help me to embrace them and share them with my peers. In Jesus' righteous name, I pray. Amen.

Grandma's Traditions

VICKIE WILSON

Train up a child in the way he should go:

and when he is old,

he will not depart from it.

Proverbs 22:6

A Balancing Act

During an early morning bus ride to work, Judith reflected upon motherhood and the many responsibilities that accompanied it. She tried very hard to balance her daily schedule of caring for her family, but many tasks were left undone. She resented her neighbor who had a clean house all the time. How did her neighbor find the time to clean and prepare meals for her family after a nine-to-five job?

Suddenly Judith remembered her grandmother, who took care of her household as well as another family. She must have been tired, but Judith couldn't recall ever hearing her complain. Am I any better than my grandmother was? If she could manage, why can't I? Before arriving at her destination, Judith made a long list of things to do that day. Topping the list was a telephone call to speak with her grandmother so that she could revive her grandmother's traditions.

Do As Grandma Did for You

She taught you how to make do
with the things you've already got.
For Grandma took a little bit
and made it be a lot.

She taught you how to love each other
including neighbors, too.
She taught you to respect your elders
or you knew what she would do.

She never gave into your wants
she provided the things you needed.
And when she gave the answer, No!
she never had to repeat it.

She walked or rode the bus to work,
cooked, cleaned, and serviced others.
But before she left for work each day
her dinner was cooked and covered.

Nourish my body with daily meals
not fending for myself.
If God provides the food for us
then you should be the chef.

WAKE UP! And learn the word
responsibility.
Grandma did these things for you,
now you should do the same for me.

Application

List the things your parents do on a daily basis for you and your siblings. Take the time today to thank them.

Prayer

Father, I am so grateful for the family traditions my parents and grandparents established. I ask that I will one day be able to pass them on to my children. Lord, give me the same strength that my grandmother and mother have shown. Amen.

Just As I Am

RAMONA TILLMAN

Being confident of this very thing,

that he which hath begun a good work

in you will perform it

until the day of Jesus Christ.

Philippians 1:6

A True Measure

Savannah was an overachiever. She had worried herself silly for As on every assignment and exam. She measured her value against the grades she received. Savannah looked forward to the first exam of the year. It would convince her that she was smart and well versed in English. Savannah was disappointed when the tests were returned and she had received a B plus. She spent the rest of class beating herself up. "Why can't I do anything right?" she said to herself. "Why didn't I get an A like I should have? Why has God let this happen to me?" The questions began to flourish until she ripped up her paper and ran out of class.

No one is perfect. All that any of us can do is press toward perfection and be the best that we can be. God is not always concerned whether we pass or fail. Although God's Word is right, just, and fair, it was written for imperfect people to follow, for us to always strive to be godly. All that is required of us is to stay in the race. Savannah was discouraged because she did not receive the grade she used to measure herself. God does not measure us in this way. He loves us just as we are, and we can trust that he will never fail us. Every situation we encounter may not work out the way we expect, but we can know that the Scripture in Philippians

1:6 is true. So never quit. God will never leave you nor forsake you.

Application

In times of disappointment, pray that God will help you to accept those things you cannot change. Finally, pray that you may be patient to wait on his deliverance. He will show himself able.

Prayer

Father, you are my Lord, my strength, and my redeemer. Thank you for your Word, which reminds me daily that you are with me in times of trouble and disappointment. When I think I have failed, show me that you accept me just as I am. Amen.

Give Your Parents a Break!

NICOLE SMITH

My son, forget not my law;

but let thine heart keep my commandments:

For length of days, and long life, and peace,

shall they add to thee.

Proverbs 3:1,2

Good Limits

Dear Aretha:

I have a serious problem. My father is unreasonably strict. I am 16, and he will not let me go places unless there is parental supervision at all times. To make matters worse, yesterday when I was dropped off at a girlfriend's house, he made my mother go to the door to meet her parents! They weren't home so I was not allowed to stay. I had to get back in the car and my parents drove me home. I have never been so embarrassed in my life. My father is the king of the household, and whatever he says, goes. He is impossible. Help!

Captive

Dear Captive:

You're cursed with parents who love you. Every teenager should have the advantages you have.

Aretha

P.S. Be assured, you will appreciate your father's "strict" attitude when you are older and become a parent.

....

Do these parents sound familiar? I hope so. Nurturing a teenager usually stirs up wrath. This time in your life may seem as if it will never end. However, your teen years will be over before you know it. I know that you don't believe it, but parenting is hard work. Give your parents a break. No matter how many siblings you may or may not have, this is your parents' first time raising you. You are growing up in a different time than they did. Each day is full of new and exciting experiences. Remember, they have a difficult task of nurturing and admonishing. Try to be obedient to them and to God's commandments to you.

Application

What can you do to help your parents? First, pray for them. Ask the Lord to bless them in all areas of their lives. Second, pray for yourself. Ask the Lord to help you be an obedient child. Third, enjoy your family; soon you will be an adult and responsible for yourself.

Prayer

Father God, I pray that my love for my parents will grow deeper each day. I realize that, as I obey them, I obey you. I realize that some girls my age do not have loving parents. I pray that you will fill that void with your perfect love. Amen.

Heeding Instructions

CHRISTINA DIXON

He is in the way of life

that keepeth instruction:

but he that refuseth reproof erreth.

Proverbs 10:17

Taking Instruction

Natalie was so tired of instructions about what and how to sing. "Diction is important when singing. Now repeat after me and sing, 'Lips, teeth, tip of the tongue . . .' On key, people!" Mrs. Burgess demonstrated for the class.

Natalie longed to sing songs with her own flavor, but Mrs. Burgess seemed to enjoy torturing the choir with scales and diction exercises. Shifting while trying hard not to fall off the riser, Natalie thought, It's the fourth week of school, for crying out loud! Who cares about proper diction anyway? Besides, this stuff is nothing like what I'm going to sing. If we have to sing "Lips, teeth, tip of the tongue" one more time, I'll scream!

Teachers who use repetition can be a pain in the neck. At times we resent folks reciting the same set of instructions to us as if we were ignorant. However, God designed us to receive awesome benefits when we embrace the reality that we need to be instructed. That's what Proverbs 10:17 teaches us. Teachers usually have our best interests at heart. They want us to reap the blessings that come from doing things with a sense of order and discipline. Order and discipline may seem like dirty words right now, especially when you may long to express your own sense of style. But before you get upset, consider the reality that your repetitive teachers could very well be blessings in disguise. You may want to take the time to thank them.

Application

Think about the things you can do—such as walking and writing—that you had to practice. You had to pull up repeatedly on legs that weren't used to walking. You had to recite and write your alphabet over and over in order to begin writing. Now you do those things without thinking about them. God designed us to learn by repetition. That's why it's important to appreciate those who consistently provide instructions. Don't forget to express your appreciation to them.

Prayer

Lord, thank you for helping me to realize that following instructions is important, and for exposing my need to embrace instruction as a way of life. In Jesus' name, I pray. Amen.

We Are Family

EVA JENISE GIBSON

As we have therefore opportunity,

let us do good unto all men,

especially unto them who are

of the household of faith.

Galatians 6:10

Give What You Can

Cameo was president of the church youth group. There were many families in the church who could not afford to buy new clothing for their children. Cameo and the youth group came up with an idea that would help these families. Each family that was able was asked to donate pieces that they were no longer using, and the items were placed in the clothes bank at church. Anyone in need of clothing could go to the bank and get what they needed for their families, free of charge.

There are many Bible stories of people helping others through giving. You may not have money to help others but you may be able to give in some other way. The Bible states in Luke 6:38, "Give, and it shall be given unto you; good measure, pressed down, and shaken together, and running over . . . it shall be measured to you again." Imagine having a lap full of blessings that are running over because of your giving.

Application

Take time today to write down ways you can help others, in the family of God and outside. You may be surprised to find that what you have to give is just what someone else is in need of. Ask God to show you ways you can supply the needs of others and to give with a willing heart. Share your list with your parents or church leader.

Prayer

Lord, help me to know when you want me to give to others. Thank you for the people you place in my life to help me make good decisions. In Jesus' name, I pray. Amen.

Try Contentment

CHANDRA SPARKS TAYLOR

Not that I speak in respect of want:

for I have learned, in whatsoever state I am,

therewith to be content.

Philippians 4:11

Take Time to Appreciate

Several years ago Brittany, a city girl through and through, moved with her parents to a small town. From the instant she set foot in the town, she hated it. The people were slow, there was nothing to do, and the kids at school already had their group of friends. She was just an outsider. She figured she would do her time there and get out when she graduated in two years. Instead of learning from her time there, every day she dreamed about leaving. She was miserable.

Eventually, in spite of herself, Brittany began to make some friends. But it was not until she learned how to be happy where she was that she was able to enjoy her life. When Brittany finally understood that God was teaching her the secret of being content, she found herself enjoying small things about the town. She became so caught up in the joys of life in a small town that, when she finally graduated, she went to college nearby so that she could come home on weekends.

Many times, we worry so much about what we don't have that we forget to take the time to appreciate what we do have. We receive so many blessings in our lives on a daily basis, but many of us fail to recognize them. Even if you feel as if you have hit rock bottom, remember that there is always someone who is worse off than you. Sometimes our worries are so great that it seems nobody can understand what we're going through, and we feel all alone. Isn't it great to know that God is always there and that we can take all of our worries to him?

Application

Keep a journal and, each day, write down five things for which you are grateful. Slowly, you will learn the secret of being content. Put aside your worries and focus on your blessings.

Prayer

Lord, thank you for all of your many blessings and for showing me the secret of being content. Amen.

Better Than Wine

MARLOW TALTON

And be not drunk with wine,

wherein is excess;

but be filled with the Spirit.

Ephesians 5:18

Drunk in the Spirit

It seemed as though all that Jasmine's homegirls wanted to do after school was to drink at the local hangout, or drink at slumber parties. Somehow she had to convince them that there was so much more to having fun than drinking alcohol. She decided to come up with a strategy to keep her friends from drinking. Julie and I attend church together and our parents have similar values, so I will use this as a way to change her mind, *she thought.* Donna is the most popular girl in our class and the one who introduced us to alcohol. I will invite her to church.

Her decision made, the next day "Operation Save My Friends" went into effect. She reminded Julie of their 17-year friendship and how both of their parents advised against such behavior. Julie asked Jasmine to forgive her for drinking. Jasmine decided to approach Donna in an unusual way by offering her a Bible and asking if she wanted to attend church. Donna agreed, and, with the encouragement of her friends, soon gave up alcohol. God had his way. The girls were drunk every Sunday from then on—but not with wine!

Being a young lady with standards and strong beliefs can bridge the barrier between peer pressure and what God has instilled in you. Do not compromise. Do not give in to peer pressure. If someone offers you a drink, offer them the best Spirit of all—God.

Application

Purchase a bottle of sparkling apple juice. Invite over your closest friends. Ask permission to use the fine crystal glasses. Toast to some of the great things going on in your lives. You'll have a blast and the fellowship between you will be the real high. And you'll show that alcohol isn't necessary to have fun.

Prayer

Dear Lord, thank you for allowing me to withstand the pressure of strong drink. Beer, wine, and other alcoholic beverages are designed to destroy the temple in me that you have created. Keep me from such and please uphold me in not compromising. Amen.

God Hates Sin

JAMELL MEEKS

To them who by patient continuance

in well doing seek for glory and honour

and immortality, eternal life:

But unto them that are contentious,

and do not obey the truth,

but obey unrighteousness, indignation

and wrath, Tribulation and anguish,

upon every soul of man that doeth evil,

of the Jew first, and also of the Gentile.

Romans 2:7-9

Turn from Sin

Jean met Andrew at school. There was an instant attraction. As they spent more time together, Jean knew that she had never met anyone as strong, smart, and funny as Andrew. He was too cute on top of it all. Jean's parents did not allow her to date because she was only 14. Jean always felt that her parents were being unfair and very old-fashioned. Andrew was 17 and had a driver's license and his own car. So every Saturday Jean would ask her parents to drop her at the mall with her friends. When they got there, Andrew was waiting for her, engine running, so they could go do something together. He would return her to the mall way before the time her parents were to pick her up, and they didn't suspect a thing.

God is not pleased with sin. When Adam and Eve first sinned in the Garden of Eden, they caused a separation between God and human beings that was only bridged by the sacrifice Jesus made on the cross. His sacrifice allows us to be forgiven for our sins. But God still hates sin.

There are many instances in the Bible where sin is defiantly repeated, and it causes God to burn with anger against the sinner. (See Deuteronomy 11:16,17 and 2 Kings 22:12,13.) But it takes a lot for our compassionate and gracious God to get to this point. He is slow to anger and, even in his anger, is quick to forgive. If you have sin in your life, don't turn away from the Lord in arrogance, defiance, or even shame. Instead, turn and face him, repent, and pray for God's blessings to keep you from more sin.

Application

Think about your own life. Is there a part of your heart that you have hidden from God? Stop now and reveal it to him. Let him work with you to get sin out of your life today.

Prayer

*Oh Lord, show me every area where I have a stronghold of
sin in my life and help me repent of it. I thank you for
your never-ending forgiveness and mercy. Amen.*

Hanging Out

TAMMY GARNES

If there come any unto you,

and bring not this doctrine,

receive him not into your house,

neither bid him God speed.

2 John 10

The Right Crowd

It was Sidney's first day in high school. Because her family had moved to a new city, she knew no one. In the hall she saw three groups of girls. One bunch wore trashy clothes and had filthy language coming from their mouths. One of those girls said, "Hey new girl, come check us out." Then there was a group with high-priced duds and uptight attitudes. One of them said, "You're new here, being with us . . . well, let's just say that we're the only group that counts." Finally there were two girls with big smiles, and they wore crosses around their necks. They greeted Sydney warmly.

It was clear to Sidney that she could be a part of any of these groups. She was down and if she wanted to, she could roll with the bad girls. She was smart and if she wanted to, she could spend time with the preppy bunch. She was also warm spirited and loved the Lord. So when she thought about which group fit her the best, she walked over to the two girls and showed them her cross.

Choosing a group of people to hang out with isn't always an easy decision. You want to be accepted and you want to have fun. Some groups look more appealing and more popular. But what if the popular group isn't interested in God? Then you need to keep looking, stand alone, or start your own group.

Make it a club that is cool and crazy for Jesus. The only cliques that make sense for you to be a part of are ones where God is included in the bunch. You need to have friends with high moral character and who accept you totally. Be careful who you want to hang out with.

Application

Write down ten attributes you want in the group you hang out with. Pray over it and refer to it often. Don't stop looking until you find a group of friends that possesses the things you want.

Prayer

Father, I want to be in the "in crowd." They're cool, and frankly, I don't want to be an outcast. However, above all, I want to be with the right crowd. Help me! Amen.

Healthy Lifestyle

PATRICE ELLIOT MACE

Beloved, I wish above all things

that thou mayest prosper

and be in health,

even as thy soul prospereth.

3 John 2

Chillin' with the Wrong Crew

It was just a few days after the new year and all Estell could think about was what wasn't right in her life. Estell's sophomore year of high school had started out fine until she decided to hang out with a new bunch of friends. Chillin' with her crew was fun. Estell never knew what they were going to get into next—like the time they went into a department store and Nikita swiped some earrings and bracelets. Estell was scared, but she thought it was kind of cool. Estell's new friends liked to smoke, drink, and party. Soon, Estell picked up her friends' habits and even passed out cold at a party from too much alcohol. By year's end, Estell's mother had to get her into a group for teens who abuse alcohol.

How did things get so messed up? Estell asked herself one morning in her bedroom. All I wanted was to have some fun and hang out with my friends. There was a knock at the door.

"Estell?" one of her old friends, Verlene, called urgently at her bedroom door, "Would you let me in? I have been trying to reach you on the phone for two weeks!" Estell forced herself to open the door.

"Estell, I know that it seems things could not be worse, but you have to remember you can turn things around from here. Let's pray that God will help you break through this difficult time," Verlene said encouragingly.

After the prayer, Estell began to feel better and said, "Thanks for coming to see about me."

"Girl, you know we go way back. We've come too far to stop now," Verlene said, smiling.

....

Our bodies must be vessels to the Lord. They must be that special place where we welcome God's presence and where his Holy Spirit dwells. Honor God by developing a healthy lifestyle that will aid your growth and development. It is your responsibility to take care of your body, a gift from God.

Application

Begin each day thanking God for the body he has provided you. Eat well and include exercise in your daily activities. Stay away from substances that would destroy your health. Become involved in activities that allow your spiritual life and self-confidence to grow.

Prayer

Most merciful and loving Father, thank you for health, strength, and countless blessings of which I will never be worthy. Help me, Lord, to honor you by caring for my mind, body, and soul. Provide me with the discipline I need to develop a healthy lifestyle. In the blessed name of Jesus, I pray. Amen.

Committed

PORTIA LEE

By whom we have received

grace and apostleship,

for obedience to the faith

among all nations, for his name.

Romans 1:5

Committed to God

Nina and Abi were best friends. They had grown up together in Sunday school and had been become Christians and were baptized around the same time. When they were both 13, Abi began hanging out with a bad crowd. One day Nina was walking past them, and one of Abi's new friends started making fun of her because she was a Christian. Abi didn't say anything, but chuckled along with the others as Nina's eyes welled up with tears. Later Abi called Nina on the phone.

"Nina, I'm so sorry. I should have said something to let them know that I am a Christian. But I was afraid they'd make fun of me, too. I felt so bad that I had to say something. When I did, they told me that I was a freak!"

"Oh, Abi, I'm glad that you changed your mind. I wasn't crying because they made fun of me. I was crying because I thought I had lost a good friend . . . and I'm sorry they made fun of you, too."

"I'm not," Abi said. "I'll be a freak any day . . . a Jesus freak." The two girls laughed.

What does it mean to be committed? Simply put, it means that your word is your bond. You pledge your allegiance to someone or something. What are you committed to? Your friends, your nice clothes, or your new car? What about being committed to your God?

Christian faith is a commitment to serving God through Jesus Christ and the Holy Spirit. Commitment means that no matter what comes or goes, you will stand for what's right in the eyes of God. Whether or not we are fully committed to God, he is faithful to us. God's not going to leave us hanging, and he will always be there for us! We should be there for him.

Application

It's the Holy Spirit who reminds us to ask the popular question, "What would Jesus do (WWJD)?" When our desire is a life committed to the service of God, we ask, listen, and do that which is appropriate because we are serving God. How do we know it is from God? We must adopt the philosophy of David in Psalm 119:11, "Thy word have I hid in mine heart, that I might not sin against thee."

Prayer

Creator God, I am blessed to have Jesus as my Savior and friend, and the Holy Spirit as my constant companion who dwells within me. Please strengthen me to listen and remain committed to you and your Word. Amen.

Lost and Found

ELOISE AVERHART

And ye shall seek me,

and find me,

when ye shall search for me

with all your heart.

Jeremiah 29:13

Never Lost to God

The gospel concert in the park ended on a high note. Betty was humming one of the songs when she heard her name called from behind her. As she turned, she saw her friend Gloria and Gloria's mother. Gloria's face seemed troubled.

"Betty, I lost my ring. When I got up from my seat to leave, it slipped off of my finger and I can't find it. That ring means a lot to me. It has sentimental value and can never be replaced. I have to find it."

Her mother said, "Gloria, why don't you search again in that opening beneath the seat." Gloria reached down and put her hand in that small dark opening, and discovered her beloved ring.

The same way that Gloria's ring slipped off her finger, we can seem to slip away from God, causing us to feel far away from him and sort of lost. It could be because we have done something wrong and need to ask God for forgiveness. Often we drift away because we don't maintain regular times of fellowship with God through prayer and Bible study.

The Word of God exhorts us to search for him with all our hearts. The word search means "to track down" and "to hunt for." As young women of God, we need that place where we can truly search for and have fellowship with our heavenly Father. This time will remind us that even though we may feel lost, we are always "found" with him.

Application

Set aside a "lost and found" place to read your Bible and pray on a regular basis. You can also listen to praise and worship music there, or read books that remind you of God's faithfulness and love. Do it today. Make it a part of your daily routine.

Prayer

Lord, you desire fellowship with me. It doesn't matter how I come to you, just that I come. Forgive the times I have stayed away, and create in me a burning desire for more of you. In Jesus' name, I pray. Amen.

Transforming Your Thoughts

EDYTHE THOMAS

Whatsoever things are true,

whatsoever things are honest,

whatsoever things are pure,

whatsoever things are lovely,

whatsoever things are of good report . . .

think on these things.

Philippians 4:8

A Mind for God

In the midst of trying to complete her homework assignment, Myiesha once again found herself lost in thoughts about Marcus. She just could not stop thinking about their most recent conversation. His words echoed in her mind, "Sweetness, I don't know anything about the things of God and truly had no interest in them until now. But if God is so important to you, maybe you can teach me a little about him. In exchange, I would be glad to teach you about the things of the world."

Myiesha fantasized that perhaps she could be the one girl in their school to settle Marcus down. Even though he was the total opposite of what she had asked God for, the more she thought on it, the more she could see being a happy couple with Marcus.

It is both natural and exciting to get lost in thoughts of dating a special boy or becoming famous, or in countless other dreams that may flood your mind. Dreams are great! They can fuel your ambition and cause you to expand your vision for life. Just be sure that whatever you are thinking about will not compromise or extinguish your passion for God.

Recognize that unholy thoughts, in the absence of repentance, become unholy actions. Be not conformed to the unholy thoughts of the world. Instead, renew your mind daily by reading God's Word. "Whatsoever things are true, whatsoever things are honest, whatsoever things are just, whatsoever things are pure, whatsoever things are lovely, whatsoever things are of good report; if there be any virtue, and if there be any praise, think on these things" (Philippians 4:8).

Application

The next time that you find yourself daydreaming, ask yourself whether or not God would be pleased with your thoughts. If the answer is no, repent of the thoughts and ask God to help transform you by renewing your mind in accordance with his will.

Prayer

Dear heavenly Father, I desire to please you in all that I say, think, and do. Please continue to conform me to your perfect will as I renew my mind through your Word. In the name of Jesus, I pray. Amen.

Mind Choices

PAMELA HUDSON

Teaching us that, denying ungodliness
and worldly lusts, we should live soberly,
righteously, and godly,
in this present world.

Titus 2:12

It's All in Your Mind

Ursula, youth captain of Leaders on the Move in her local church, loved movies and collected the latest releases. She had such a large collection that she was a gold star member at the corner video store. Ursula paid little attention to the movie guild's rating describing what type of movie she was purchasing. If she liked a movie and if one of her favorite actors was in it, she bought it.

Deanne had recently moved from California to Ursula's church. Ursula invited Deanne over to watch movies, excited that she might be gaining a new friend who would like her passion for movies. When Deanne saw her video collection, she voiced her concern about the time that Ursula was spending watching R-rated movies. "You know, the profanity, sexual content, and adult themes are affecting your mind, don't you?" Deanne remarked.

"It's just entertainment; that's all—no harm done." While Ursula was hurt, the words stirred her. Nevertheless, she decided that she would not share her movies with Deanne again.

One Sunday, the youth pastor preached about how our minds are like computers. He said that we retain all that's put in our minds—negative and unbiblical images. He preached that what goes in our minds will produce the ugliness of sin in our lives.

Wow, Ursula thought, *what do they expect me to do with my video collection?*

....

We say we are born-again Christians and that Jesus is our Lord and Savior, but our hobbies sometimes don't reflect the holiness of Christ. Decide today that your entertainment will uplift your spiritual thought life and not take from it.

Application

Make a list of your recreational activities. Label each "godly" or "ungodly." Begin to eliminate the ungodly ones from your list and from your life. It may take some time, but the spiritual rewards are worth it.

Prayer

Heavenly Father, forgive me for not taking better care of my mind. I have not regarded the things I feed into my mind, and I have willfully participated in activities that might lead to sin. Help me to make more godly choices in everything. In Jesus' name, I pray. Amen.

Lead by Example

KIM BAILEY

Be not deceived: evil communications

corrupt good manners.

1 Corinthians 15:33

Witness in Word and Deed

"Girl, you ain't heard a word I said," Nana snapped, one hand on her hip, eyeing Joleen.

"Sorry, Nana, I'm listening . . . and thinking. I'm just trying to figure out what to do."

"Far as I'm concerned, ain't no two ways about it. Your friend Danielle stole that candy bar. That makes her a thief—period!"

"But it's not that simple," Joleen said. *"Danielle didn't intend to steal. It was a joke at first. She was just kidding around. By the time we reached the door, she saw the owner staring and panicked. Then she slipped it into my book bag,"* Joleen explained.

"Are you making excuses for that girl again?"

....

Do you go along with others just to satisfy them? Or do you speak up when something is not right? Bad behavior is bad behavior, no matter how we try to justify it. Decisions about who we spend our time with and what activities we participate in can have a positive or negative influence on our lives. Peer pressure has been cited as one of the main reasons why teens participate in wrongdoing, even when they know better. Perhaps you've silenced your words while observing something that is obviously wrong. Maybe you think you're being a good friend by laughing or shrugging off inappropriate behavior.

As Christians, it is our divine duty to lead by example. Witnessing involves more than just telling others about right and wrong according to God's Word. As opportunities arise, you also can share how living by God's principles has changed your life. Be honest about your challenges and vulnerabilities, so that people know you're human, too. Share with others in such a way that it leaves them wanting to know more about God.

Application

Today observe your own behavior, attitudes, moods, and beliefs. What do you see? If you discover that your actions or words are out of line, make a decision to change. Find ways to correct yourself for your own sake as well as for the sake of others.

Prayer

Father God, I want to be a witness for you in word and deed. When I am faced with difficult situations that challenge my beliefs, help me to make the right decisions—the ones that honor you. Amen.

Walking by Faith

PAMELA ROLLINS

For we walk by faith, not by sight.

2 Corinthians 5:7

Behind-the-Scenes Faith

Tina rushed onto the stage and set some props in place. As head of props for the youth-group play, she was responsible for setting things up. When the performance ended, Tina finished her work and picked up her jacket. She gave a big sigh as she walked down the steps of the church.

Miss Jacob met her. "Congratulations on the fine job you did on the play! But why the big sigh? Are you tired?"

"Yeah, I guess so," Tina nodded. "Tired, and discouraged about some other stuff."

"Care to talk about it?" asked Miss Jacob.

Tina shrugged, but then she shared her concerns about her aunt. Tina's aunt, who lived with them, was not a Christian. Tina dearly loved her aunt and was afraid that she would be lost for all eternity. "Mom and I have prayed and prayed for Aunt Laura," Tina said, "but it hasn't done any good."

"Wait a minute, Tina," said Miss Jacob. "How do you know your prayers haven't done any good? How do you know your aunt is the same? Have faith."

Tina was surprised. "I sure don't see any change," she said.

. . . .

Believing in the unseen is sometimes hard for us to do. As soon as we pray we expect to see results. But you can't see inside someone's heart. God could be doing a work that we can't see on the outside.

Think about the play that Tina worked so hard on. The audience couldn't see all the behind-the-scenes work that took place to make it a success. God often does a lot of behind-the-scenes work, too, before there are any visible results. Our prayers and our witness are part of the unseen things that will bring final results. We must believe in the things we cannot see.

Application

Today think about the times when God has moved in your life, even though it took a while before others noticed a visible change.

Prayer

God, help me to keep believing in you, believing that whatever I ask of you—in your will—it will be done. Even when it looks as if there is no change, I know that you are working. In Jesus' name, I pray. Amen.

The Test

VERONICA ALEXANDER

Examine me, O LORD,

and prove me; try my reins

and my heart.

Psalm 26:2

No Test, No Testimony

The bell rang. Mr. Morris stepped into the classroom, grabbed a stack of papers from his desk, and began passing them out. "I was very disappointed that no one in this class made an A on this test; the highest score was an 87," he said.

Mr. Morris gave Sabrina her paper. The grade was written in red ink. A 73? For a moment, Sabrina sat staring in disbelief, and then she quickly covered her paper to hide her grade. She had studied more for this test than any test she had ever taken, and she had prayed to do well. Her throat hurt as the tears choked her. How could this happen to her? In the past God had always brought her through, but where was he today?

"Uh-hmmm," Mr. Morris interrupted her thoughts by clearing his throat. The classroom grew quiet and Mr. Morris continued, "This will be the first and last time that I will offer such leniency. I am going to give each of you the opportunity to add 13 points to your test score by completing a take-home assignment."

When things look their worst, they can only get better. Nothing is impossible with God, and nothing is too hard for God (Luke 1:37). When you are put to the test and the results aren't what you have hoped for, remember that God makes a way out of no way! When things look bad, remember that God has not left you (Hebrew 13:5). He is right there in the situation, working on your behalf. You just do your part, put forth your best effort, and watch God do the rest. Without a test you wouldn't have a testimony!

Application

Discuss with your parents the tests that you have, both in and out of school. Ask them to pray with you. Be sure to share the answers to your prayers with them, and to thank God for the outcomes.

Prayer

Lord, let me work hard to do my best and to trust that you are going to see me through. Please help me to remember that you make a way out of no way. Today I will trust you to give me the victory. Amen.

Quiet Time

MARILYN TURNER

Come ye yourselves apart

into a desert place, and rest a while.

> *Mark 6:31*

Take Time

"Rise and shine, my sunflowers, a new day is dawning! I've got to take the car to the shop after I drop you off at school and I can't afford to be late. So no lollygagging, fussing, or fighting. And I mean it."

Charmayne groaned inwardly. At 6:00 A.M. Mom's chronically cheerful voice was downright irritating. "First dibs on the bathroom," her younger sister yelled, springing out of bed and darting into the coveted room. "Your turn to walk the dog, Charmayne!" her brother reminded her.

Great, no hot water for me this morning, Charmayne thought. Sighing, Charmayne sat upright in her bed, sending her history book crashing to the floor. She moaned, remembering that she'd fallen asleep studying for today's history exam. Five minutes into her day and she was stressed already.

William Penn once said, "True silence is the rest of the mind and is to the spirit what sleep is to the body, nourishment and refreshment." The need to rest our minds is logical, but finding silence, solitude, and peace is tough. Even when we find a place that is quiet, our noisy, nagging thoughts can make true silence impossible.

In order to really communicate with God, that is to speak to and hear from him, we must make a choice. We must choose to step away from the distractions of everyday living in order to step into the presence of God. Throughout the Gospels, we find Jesus choosing to steal away from the "busyness" of life in order to hear from his Father. Are you willing to follow Jesus' example?

Application

Read Mark 6:30-32. Picture yourself with Jesus and the disciples, getting into the boat to find some quiet time. Think about sitting beside a smiling and relaxed Jesus as the warm sun shines down on your face while your boat glides across the smooth, blue sea. Think about how peaceful and quiet you feel as Jesus freely and lovingly converses with you about all the concerns that are in your heart. What is Jesus saying to you? Take a moment to write down his words. Are they judgmental or angry? Of course not! Jesus loves you and wants to share time with you. Use this exercise often; it will help to remind you of the value of being quiet with God.

Prayer

Lord, when the thoughts in my mind and the noise of my environment are screaming for attention, please help me to be still and quiet. Allow me to hear from you. Thank you, Jesus, for letting your quiet presence into my heart. Amen.

What's a Church?

GWEN COATES

Blessed are they that dwell in thy house:

they will be still praising thee.

Psalm 84:4

Give Church a Chance

This was not the way a church was supposed to look! A storefront building with a couple of pews and all kinds of chairs—folding chairs, wooden chairs, and even dining-room-table chairs. The heater was hanging from the ceiling in the back corner of the building, and when the blower came on, you couldn't hear anything else.

It didn't look like a church, but it sure did act like one. There was Sunday school, church service, Wednesday night prayer meeting, Bible study, and choir practice. The pastor even organized a group of other storefront churches to "fellowship" at a different church once a month. The members learned to do everything. If the deacons didn't show up, the youth would lead devotions. If the teachers didn't show up, someone would pitch in to teach Sunday school. If the janitor didn't show up, some of the members would take off their hats and get down on their knees to clean. The teenagers sang in the choir, memorized Scripture, and fellowshipped with other youth groups. It wasn't that bad. But it sure didn't look like a church.

Sometimes we are so worried about the outward appearance of a church that we often miss the lessons we can learn within its walls. Where is it written that a church has to have cushioned pews, a center aisle, and a baptismal pool? Church is in your heart;

the place where you attend is secondary. Your first priority is to make sure that whatever your church looks like, God is in the midst.

Application

Give church a chance. This Sunday, visit the church of your choice, whether it's a storefront or the kind of building many of us have come to associate with church. Many of life's lessons are learned in the house of God with the family of God.

Prayer

Lord, I thank you for the many houses of worship that are open in your name. Allow me to get beyond looking at the building so I can focus on you. In Jesus' name. Amen.

God's Beauty Mark

LAVERNE HALL

And God saw every thing that he had made,

and, behold, it was very good.

Genesis 1:31

God Made You

It was Friday night at the Johnsons' house and they were in the midst of celebrating Jennifer's thirteenth birthday. As Jennifer was preparing to blow out the candles, her little brother, George, looked at her and sang, "Thirteen and still ugly, thirteen and still ugly. Big eyes, big lips, and a big nose in between. Thirteen and still ugly!" Mom and Dad had to intervene as Jennifer was about to reach across the table and grab her little brother. Everybody ate cake and ice cream and ended up having a good time.

Once in her room though, Jennifer reflected as she looked at herself in the mirror. Just like her little brother said, "big eyes, big lips and a big nose in between." Her skin color didn't make it any better; she was neither really light nor really dark. She was an in-between mousy brown. And her hair was not really pretty either. You know, she thought, everybody couldn't be all wrong. I really must be ugly. She took one last look in the mirror, and then cried herself to sleep.

In the beginning God created the heavens and the earth, and he fashioned man and woman in his image. After his work was finished, he looked at all he had created and said, "That's good!" With tender loving thought, God made you, too. He shaped and shaded you from the sparkling dust of nature, sprinkled with gold dust, and gave you your unique lips, hair, and beautiful rich color. Be happy with the way you look, knowing that you are one of God's natural beauty marks.

Application

Look in the mirror today and instead of wishing you could change what you see, thank God for being his beautiful daughter.

Prayer

Dear Father, thank you for making me a unique creation.
With each word I utter, I pray your Spirit in my speech.
With each smile I show, I pray your sparkle in my glow.
With each deed that I do, I pray your will be done. Amen.

Joy

MARSHA WOODARD

Then was our mouth filled with laughter,

and our tongue with singing.

Psalm 126:2

Overflowing Joy

The football game was a close one. It seemed that the team would lose, but the cheerleaders kept shouting and the crowd kept cheering and the minutes seemed to be suspended. This was the most intense game of the season, and Melissa, Jessica, and Kenya thought they would run out of cheers before the whistle blew. Suddenly Robert got the ball and ran 60 yards and made the touchdown! The crowd exploded into screams.

Later that evening as they gathered at the shack, the excitement could be heard and felt in the air. Contagious laughter rang out, and joy filled the group as they talked about their victory that day.

Life is more than a football game, but sports help us to see what emotions and excitement look like. When a game is close and our team wins, we shout with enthusiastic joy. For days just thinking about the game brings smiles to our faces.

We should be as joyous in our faith walk as we are after our favorite team wins a sporting event. Many of the psalms are examples of how God's people showed their joy when God gave them a victory. Often they were so full of joy that they could not contain it, but had to open their mouths and let it come spilling out.

Application

This week be on the lookout for a time when you see God's deliverance in some area. When that happens, open up your mouth and shout for joy. Start a new tradition in your school—be a joy spreader.

Prayer

God, please help me be as joyous when you move in my life as I am when my favorite team wins. Fill my mouth with joyous laughter and help me to praise your name. Amen.

Kindness

NICOLE BAILEY WILLIAMS

But after that the kindness and love of God

our Saviour toward man appeared;

Not by works of righteousness

which we have done,

but according to his mercy

he saved us.

Titus 3:4,5

Loyal Love

Niece visited Mrs. Lola twice a week at Maranatha Residential Home. She walked into the area where the residents were playing cards, singing, and having conversation. Mrs. Lola was sitting all alone in her wheelchair. Mrs. Lola was seldom asked to join in anything because she had a temper that no one could bear. But that didn't stop Niece.

"Hi Mrs. Lola," said Niece.

Mrs. Lola squirmed. "I wish you would go away," she said. "I don't know why you even bother coming here."

"I bother because I care about you, Mrs. Lola," Niece replied.

"I don't see why. Everyone else says I'm a grouchy old woman."

"Well Mrs. Lola, grouchy old women need kindness, too. And besides you're not that bad. I enjoy being around you. Over the months I have learned so much by visiting you."

What is lovingkindness? It is loyal love, an attribute of God's character that is seen in how he deals with his people. God's anger is for a moment, but his loyal love is forever.

God's lovingkindness is a part of his mercy, and his mercy accepts and blesses us when we deserve to be totally rejected.

God wants us to be kind to others as a part of our Christian growth. Only as we allow the Holy Spirit to control our lives, can we experience this working in us. Left to ourselves, we sometimes find it hard to be kind. But when we surrender to the Holy Spirit and trust the Lord to work through us, we then become what God wants us to be.

Application

Look at different situations in your life where you have been unkind, and try to begin showing kindness. This will help you in building your spirit.

Prayer

Father God, help me to yield to the Spirit inside and to use every situation in my life as a way to grow. Teach me how to show lovingkindness to everyone I come in contact with. In Jesus' name. Amen.

Peace

ADELL DICKINSON

Grace and peace be multiplied unto you

through the knowledge of God,

and of Jesus our Lord.

2 Peter 1:2

Perfect Peace

Kyra sat at the kitchen table confused, agitated, and full of fear. She was so bewildered by what had happened. Her peaceful world was shattered and turned upside down. She could hardly believe that just a week ago life had been wonderful. She had lots of friends, the cutest boy in school had just asked her for a date, and school, well it was okay too. Life was just about perfect.

Then the terrorist attack happened on September 11, and now death, terror, war, and fear were all she could see and hear. Kyra had cried, along with her friends, as she watched the horrible tragedy on television. "Lord, will I ever know peace again? Will things ever be the same again?"

When it seems as if our world is spinning out of control, it is good to know the God who made the world. He has it all in control, and our life and peace are in his hands—not in the hands of terrorists. God's peace comes to us through the knowledge of his Word. He will keep us in perfect peace if we meditate on the Word and will multiply his peace to us as we grow in our knowledge of him. The equation is simple: the more we know about God, the more peace we will have.

Application

You must get to know God! Know his power, his promises, and his great love for you. Today, take time to learn what Jesus has to say about anything that disrupts your peace. Then take what you have learned and apply it to your situation.

Prayer

Father, I thank you for loving me and keeping my life in your hands. I trust you to keep me in perfect peace when there is confusion all around me. Amen.

Control
Yourself

KAREN WADDLES

Blessed are the meek:

for they shall inherit the earth.

Matthew 5:5

Taming the Wild Horse

Ebony was totally out of control. She'd been rude to her parents and teachers and hardly had any friends because she was so unpredictable. One moment she was calm and coolheaded, and the next she was mad at the world. No one really knew how unhappy she was with herself because of her inability to keep it together.

The Bible has a lot to say about self-control. In the Sermon on the Mount, Jesus spoke of the attitudes that Christians should have, and one of them is meekness. He said that those who are meek are blessed, or happy. Meekness is "bridled strength" or "strength under control." Picture this: A rancher takes a wild horse and trains it until he tames that wild spirit. He then places a harness around its neck and a bit in its mouth. The horse still has incredible strength, but it is now manageable and under control. This is meekness.

Before you became a Christian you were just like that wild horse—totally out of control. Maybe you even feel that way now. You let your passions, emotions, likes, and dislikes control your actions. But there is wonderful news! The work of the Holy Spirit in your life is to bring those emotions and passions under control, so that we demonstrate a life overflowing with Christ's character.

Application

Every time you enter a new situation today, such as changing classes, meeting someone new, having a new conversation, or a social event, stop to take a moment to invite the Holy Spirit along.

Prayer

Lord Jesus, sometimes I feel so out of control. I ask your Holy Spirit to help me learn how to allow you to tame my spirit so that I am truly meek. Help me to bring every area of my life under your control. In Jesus' name. Amen.

Real Knowledge

CHANDRA DIXON

When wisdom entereth into thine heart,

and knowledge is pleasant unto thy soul;

Discretion shall preserve thee.

Proverbs 2:10,11

Life Lessons

It was Jessica's junior year in college, and she was so excited about graduating the following year. Her hard work was finally about to pay off. Jessica had learned so much in her three years in college. Although there were more good times than bad times, she could always count on a struggle or two each semester. Many times she had thought she would be overcome by the difficulty she encountered, but her faith in God always pulled her through.

Now, as she looked back on these trying times, they really did not seem that bad. Each trial and tribulation actually made Jessica a better person. She had learned a life lesson during and after each crisis. Jessica finally understood how college years prepared her for womanhood. They provided the knowledge needed for her to become a doctor one day, and wisdom to handle life's other challenges along the way.

People often talk about going to college to get an education. But when we think of this type of education, we are usually thinking of curriculum courses. We must understand that college provides a life education as well. We learn more about friendships, hardships, and perseverance. Continue to hunger and strive for this kind of knowledge. The life knowledge that you obtain is something that can never be taken away. Proverbs 3:13 says, "Happy is the [woman] that findeth wisdom, and the [woman] that getteth understanding."

Learn a lesson from each destination in life's journey. Take with you knowledge that God has provided in order to make you a better person. Think back on life's lessons today and recall what you have learned.

Application

Take a walk around your school and pray for your journey there to be filled with new wisdom and understanding.

Prayer

Dear Lord, I come to you today with bowed head and open heart, asking you to continue to grant me wisdom and knowledge to make my paths straight. I will continue to lean on your understanding and will trust in you with all of my heart. Thank you Lord, for all your blessings. Amen.

Single and
Whole

RAYKEL TOLSON

And he said unto her,

Daughter, thy faith hath made thee whole;

go in peace, and be whole of thy plague.

Mark 5:34

True Wholeness

"Wasn't that a lovely wedding? Sharon's dress was beautiful, and she looked so happy," Great-Aunt Bertha commented.

"Yes, it was a lovely wedding," Tracy responded.

"Tracy, baby, didn't seeing your younger cousin walk down the aisle inspire you to find a nice young man to marry?" Great-Aunt Sally Mae patted Tracy's hand.

Before Tracy could answer, Great-Aunt Bertha said, "Don't worry Tracy, you'll be next. You will find your other half very soon."

"I sure hope so, because you aren't getting any younger. You'll be 30 this year, won't you?" Great-Aunt Sally Mae looked at Tracy with sympathy.

....

Too often people view being single as some kind of disease. Many think that there is something wrong with a woman older than 30 who has never been married. Do not define your singleness as a season you have to endure, alone and lonely. Instead, define being single as being separate, unique, and whole.

Separate means being "set apart." In 2 Corinthians 6:17 we are admonished to "come out from among them, and be ye separate." Unique is defined as "being the only one; remarkable, and rare."

Psalms 139:14 says we are "fearfully and wonder-fully made." Whole is defined as "not broken or damaged; something complete in itself." In Mark 5:34, Jesus told the woman with the issue of blood that her faith in God had made her whole.

Too many single women think that they will be made whole if they get married or have a relationship. Wrong! All throughout the gospels we read about Jesus telling people that their faith has made them whole. He does not refer to their marital status.

Application

Today, take time to celebrate what makes you the unique, young woman you are. Also, make a list of the areas where you feel that you are not whole (e.g., if you were wronged by a loved one and have not gotten over it; suffer from depression or low self-esteem, etc.). After you have completed the list, pray the prayer below. Do this every day until you feel whole.

Prayer

Father, I thank you for being whole, nothing missing and nothing broken. I thank you that you will use my season of singleness as a time for healing and restoration. I thank you for the blood of Jesus that makes me whole. In the name of Jesus, I am whole. Amen.

Temptation

FRANCIS JEFFERSON

Pray that ye enter not into temptation.

Luke 22:40

Temptations Await You

Terry's reward for learning how to type excellent business letters was a telephone call from the personnel manager at the local bank. Terry was hired as a drive-thru teller after the bank manager had received Terry's letter and looked at her qualifications. The job, while starting at minimum wage, would help her to save money for her own car and a nice apartment.

On Terry's first day on the job, she met Susan, and they soon became friends. The two ate lunch together every day and even started spending some weekend time together at Susan's beautiful new apartment. Terry spoke admirably about Susan's apartment. Susan told her that she could have an apartment a whole lot faster if Terry pushed to the side 75 cents or less of every deposit involving change. Susan said clients did not miss small change and that it was very easy to do. All Terry had to do was tell the client that he or she had made a small error in addition. Susan said her first month doing the "change thing" netted her 60 dollars extra.

The possibility of experiencing independent living in an apartment of your own and having an automobile can be exciting. When beginning a new job and working for minimum wage, it is difficult to be patient. Realize that it may take time to accomplish all that you would like. As a child of God, you must go back to the Lord's Prayer, particularly the verse that says, "And lead us not into temptation, but deliver us from evil" (Matthew 6:13).

Make sure that you are not working for all the wrong reasons. You must remember that the opportunity to be employed is not a given, but a gift. Look around you and see all of the unemployment. Your ethic should reflect your appreciation of God's gift to you. In return, you should live up to the commitment made when you accepted the employer/employee relationship. "Pray that ye enter not into temptation" (Luke 22:40). If you yield to temptation, you are saying that you don't really trust God, and that you cannot be trusted with his gift of a job.

Application

As you start your day, pause to consider possible distractions that may influence you to yield to temptation. Write down Luke 22:40 on an index card and carry it with you. Pray for strength not to fall into temptation.

Prayer

Father, I have some weaknesses. I ask that you will keep your arms of love wrapped around me so that I may be strengthened and guided by you in tempting situations. In the name of the victory of your Son, Jesus Christ! Amen.

The Master Planner

CHERRILL WILSON

For I know the thoughts that I think

toward you, saith the LORD,

thoughts of peace, and not of evil,

to give you an expected end.

Jeremiah 29:11

God Has Good Plans

The challenges of middle school were hard but fun. Now it was time for high school, and Chantel was nervous. Mom and Dad wanted Chantel to go to the high school in the neighborhood. It was a good academic school, but it did not specialize in the vocation that she desired. She had made plans to become a beautician. Ever since Chantel was a toddler she had a knack for doing hair. She loved combing her dolls' hair and would line them up to work on their hair as though they were in the beauty salon.

The high school she wanted was not located in the best of neighborhoods. The time had come to have a heart-to-heart talk with Mom and Dad about this important decision. Prayerfully, Chantel hoped that her parents would listen and then allow her to go to the school of her choice.

Planning for high school is a crucial part of growing up. Parents want the best for their sons and daughters, especially as their children are transitioning into the teenage years. They sometimes make decisions, and it appears that the teenager's thoughts or wishes are ignored. With spiritual guidance, love, and respect for each other's opinions (parent and teenager), the proper decision can be made.

Ultimately, God is the Master Planner of our lives. He knew when we were born, where we are now, and what the future holds for us. It is important to consult the Lord about all of our decisions. With his guidance, he will lead us in the right direction. Just as parents want what is best for their children, God desires the best for his children.

Application

Stop for a moment and think about the plans that you have made for the next several months. Have you included God in your plans? Have you prayed about your strategy? If you did, good for you! If you didn't, then take time to pray and consult Jesus about the plans that you have. Confide in him from the very beginning and you cannot go wrong.

Prayer

Dear Jesus, you are the Master Planner, so guide my thoughts with your Word, for I belong to you. My plans can only be perfected if you take control of my life. Amen.

Serving God

MICHELE CLARK JENKINS

And now, Israel, what doth the LORD

thy God require of thee,

but to fear the LORD thy God,

to walk in all his ways, and to love him,

and to serve the LORD thy God

with all thy heart and with all thy soul.

Deuteronomy 10:12

God's Will

Cathy was making her way up the career ladder at the Christian bookstore where she worked. She was next in line for promotion to manager. The hours were long with changing shifts and her feet were often tired, but it was her chosen profession. She loved that she always had Sundays off to go to church. She knew that God had called her to the ministry several years ago, but life just hadn't taken her in that direction yet, and until it did (and she had saved up some money), that "dream" would just have to wait. Meanwhile she was serving people at the bookstore by selling them Christian materials and witnessing to them whenever they asked questions about being a Christian.

....

In all your good works are you serving God or other people? When we serve God, we don't decide the path of our life all on our own. We ask him to shed light on our path like a lamp unto our feet. There is a big difference between doing what we want for ourselves or what others ask of us, and serving God by doing his will. God has a great and wonderful plan for each of our lives if we will just seek him out to find what it is.

Application

Wake up early in the morning, before anyone else in your house is awake. Don't utter a word, just meditate on asking the Lord to show you how you can serve him and know his will. Don't pray for anyone or anything else, just that one request. Then listen quietly, and write down anything you receive during this quiet time.

Prayer

Lord, I surrender my life to you and I will be obedient to your will in my life. Use me, Lord, as a tool to bring others closer to you by acts of service to them. Amen.

Another Chance

PATRICIA HEGGLER

This is the day which the LORD hath made;

we will rejoice and be glad in it.

Psalm 118:24

Each New Day

The car began to skid and then it flipped over—one, two, three times. For a few moments there was only darkness and silence. Then the sound of an oncoming car broke the quiet. Suddenly there were footsteps and a voice was saying, "Hello! Are you hurt?" Four weeping cries could be heard, and one voice yelled, "We are okay, but we're trapped!"

A man instructed the teenagers to cover their faces, and if possible, move away from the windows. The unknown rescuer went back to his car and returned to the wreckage with a tire iron. After one good swing the rear window shattered. All four young ladies climbed free of the wreckage without a scratch, and marveled at how an evening of fun almost had a tragic ending.

Many times we take life for granted, expecting to wake up every morning as usual. We jump out of bed, get ready for the day ahead, and keep moving. God is not even thought of. Sometimes when things are not going too well in our lives—we break up with a boyfriend, we're failing a class, or we're not getting along with friends—we would prefer not to wake up. But each day offers us new opportunities to clean up where we have messed up. Every day that we are alive is another chance to make things better—another opportunity to get it right!

The death angel can come at any time, no matter now old or how young we are. So we have to be thankful for each and every day that we are alive.

Application

Fold a sheet of notebook paper in half. On one side of the fold write down something you did yesterday that you would like to do better today. Pray and ask God for guidance. Then write on the other side of the fold a way you can correct yesterday's failure so it can become today's success.

Prayer

Oh God, thank you for waking me up this morning and allowing me to see a new day. Thank you for another chance at life, and another chance to get it right. Amen.

The Promised Gift

RACHELLE HOLLIE GUILLORY

Then Peter said unto them,

Repent, and be baptized every one of you

in the name of Jesus Christ

for the remission of sins,

and ye shall receive the gift

of the Holy Ghost.

Acts 2:38

God's Holy Spirit

Ever since she was a toddler, Ernestine went to church with her parents. She attended Sunday school and she even went to midweek Bible study. But when she reached 16, she did not feel as if she belonged at the church. She felt a void and thought there had to be something more to church than just listening to the choir and the sermon each week. Britni asked Ernestine if she had the Holy Spirit in her life.

"No," Ernestine responded. "I didn't know I could have it like other people. What do I need to do?"

"It's a gift, it's free," Britni told her. "All you need to do is believe in Jesus as your Lord and Savior, and you will receive the Holy Spirit. It's promised to you."

There is no greater gift to receive than the gift of God's Spirit. The Holy Ghost is the comfort, guide, and sustainer of those counted among the body of Christ. When we do not know what or how to pray, the Holy Spirit will spiritually speak for us in ways that our natural mouths could never utter (Romans 8:26). The Holy Spirit is our intercessor as well. We need this gift in order to successfully walk the daily Christian walk.

Application

Today, when you encounter a friend or just someone you happen to share a ride with on the bus, share the good news of God's gift with them. If you have not received this promised treasure, search the Scriptures and discover how you can enjoy salvation through Christ.

Prayer

Father, please fill me with your Holy Spirit. I recognize that I need your Spirit to help me live the Christian life. Help me share the good news about this precious gift with others. In your name, I pray. Amen.

How's Your Vision?

TREVY MCDONALD

Where there is no vision,

the people perish:

but he that keepeth the law,

happy is he.

Proverbs 29:18

What's Next?

"I'm so happy to see you," Michelle said as she hugged her 13-year-old cousin Ashley, who was visiting from Tennessee. "I can hardly believe you're going to high school; it seems like just yesterday you were born," Michelle said, looking at Ashley. "So what's next? After high school, what do you want to be when you grow up?"

"I'm not sure."

"What do you like to do?"

"Well, back home my friends and I like to listen to music and write stories, that's all."

"Well, my dear," Michelle said as she put Ashley's bags in the trunk of her car, "you gotta have a vision, set some goals for your life, and now is the time to start."

Decisions, decisions, decisions. It's hard enough trying to decide what dress to wear for Youth Sunday, and now everyone is bombarding you with questions about the rest of your life. You feel that you have plenty of time to decide and that you'll probably change your mind if you choose something now, right?

While your interests may change from time to time in your life, you must prepare for the future. And that preparation starts with having a vision. Proverbs 29:18 says, "Where there is no vision, the people perish." How can you move forward if you don't know which direction you are headed? But those with a plan know where they are going. Remember, having a vision doesn't mean having a detailed road map for every aspect of your life, but rather having a dream, a goal, an ambition to which you aspire.

Application

In your quiet time, take a moment to think about your future. What do you want to do? Where do you want to be in the next five years? In the next ten years? If you haven't already, write down your goals and ask yourself, "What can I do now to help me reach them?"

Prayer

Dear heavenly Father, thank you for the many ways you have blessed my life. Lord, give me your vision for my life, and make it clear so that I can prepare for my future. In Jesus' name. Amen.

Topical Index

Church 149
Commitment 117
Contentment 97
Convictions 13, 129
Devotions 121, 145
Disappointment 81
Entertainment 129
Faith 137
Forgiveness 65
Friendship 21, 109
God's Love 9, 61
God's Plan 45, 185, 189
Guys 25
Health 113
Joy 157
Kindness 161
Marriage 73

Obedience 49, 69, 89
Parents 49, 77, 85
Peace 165
Peer Pressure 101, 109, 133
Privacy 53
Self-Image 153
Serving God 189
Serving Others 93
Sex 33, 37
Sin 30, 105
Success 17
Thankfulness 97
Thoughts 5, 125, 129
The Tongue 41, 133
Values 57

The Wisdom and Grace Devotional BIBLE

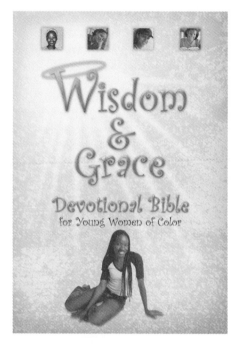

If you enjoyed this brief book, you will love the *Wisdom and Grace Devotional Bible for Young Women of Color*. Twelve months of devotions appear in full color in the King James Bible. Each devotional includes an opening story, devotional thought, application, and prayer. It will take you through a whole year of growing closer to God!